D1208608

# Guess Who
# Stings

## Dana Meachen Rau

**Marshall Cavendish**
Benchmark
New York

I can fly.

I have four wings.

I can fly up and down.

I can fly side to side.

I have five eyes.

I look for flowers.

I find a good flower.

I dance to tell others.

I drink from flowers.

My tongue is like a straw.

I have six legs.

I have hair on my body.

I have two *antennas*.

They help me smell and touch.

I live in a busy *hive*.

The hive looks like a box.

The hive is filled with *honeycomb*.

The honeycomb has little holes.

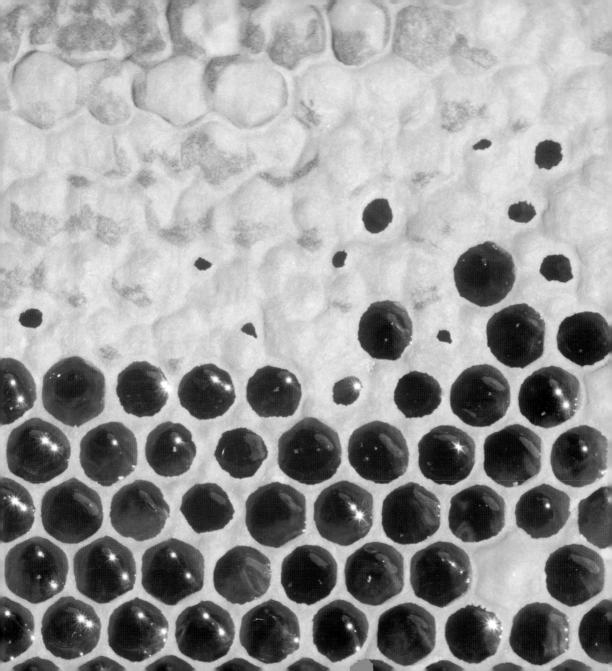

The honeycomb holds honey.

The honeycomb holds eggs.

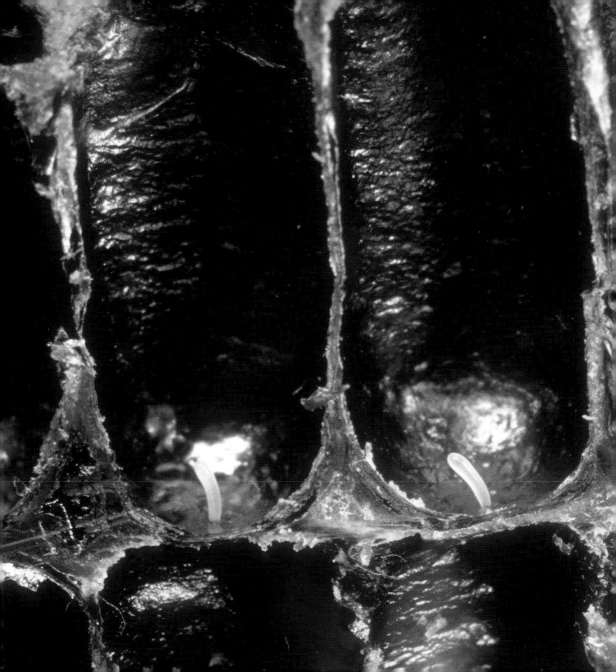

The eggs turn into *grubs*.

Grubs turn into grownups.

I sting if you scare me.

Who am I?

I am a honeybee!

# Who am I?

**antennas**

**eyes**

**grubs**

**hive**

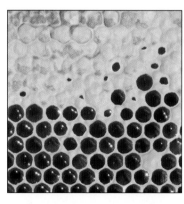
**honeycomb**

**tongue**

**wings**

# Challenge Words

**antennas** (an-TEN-uhs) A pair of long, thin feelers on a honeybee's head.

**grubs** The short, fat worms from a honeybee's eggs.

**hive** A box or other shelter for honeybees.

**honeycomb** (HUN-ee-kohm) The small wax holes in a hive that hold honey and eggs.

# Index

Page numbers in **boldface** are illustrations.

## About the Author

Dana Meachen Rau is the author of many other titles in the Bookworms series, as well as other nonfiction and early reader books. She lives in Burlington, Connecticut, with her husband and two children.

With thanks to the Reading Consultants:

Nanci Vargus, Ed.D., is an Assistant Professor of Elementary Education at the University of Indianapolis.

Beth Walker Gambro is an Adjunct Professor at the University of St. Francis in Joliet, Illinois.

Marshall Cavendish Benchmark
99 White Plains Road
Tarrytown, New York 10591-5502
www.marshallcavendish.us

Text copyright © 2009 by Marshall Cavendish Corporation

Library of Congress Cataloging-in-Publication Data

Rau, Dana Meachen, 1971–
Guess who stings / by Dana Meachen Rau.
p. cm. — (Bookworms. Guess who)
Summary: "Following a guessing game format, this book provides young readers with
clues about a honeybee's physical characteristics, behaviors, and habitats, challenging readers
to identify it"—Provided by publisher.
Includes index.
ISBN 978-0-7614-2973-9
1. Honeybee—Juvenile literature. I. Title. II. Series.
QL568.A6R38 2009
595.79'9—dc22
2007024612

Editor: Christina Gardeski
Publisher: Michelle Bisson
Designer: Virginia Pope
Art Director: Anahid Hamparian

Photo Research by Anne Burns Images

Cover Photo by *Alamy Images*/Phototake

The photographs in this book are used with permission and through the courtesy of:
*Animals Animals*: pp. 1, 19, 28BR Donald Specker; p. 9 Stephen Dalton.
*Alamy Images*: pp. 3, 29R Chris Mole. *Corbis*: p. 5 David Stobbe/Reuters;
pp. 11, 29L Fritz Rauschenback/zefa; p. 25 Lynda Richardson.
*Dwight Kuhn Photography*: pp. 7, 13, 23, 28TC&TR. *Photo Researchers*: pp. 15, 28TL Darwin Dale;
pp. 17, 28BL Ken Cavanagh. *PhototakeUSA*: p. 21 Scott Carnazine. *Charles Melton*: p. 27.

Printed in Malaysia
1  3  5  6  4  2